The People We Love

To order additional copies, please contact us.
BookSurge, LLC
www.booksurge.com
1-866-308-6235
orders@booksurge.com

The People We Love

Stories and Poems of Love and Devotion

Hunter Street Elementary School's
First and Second Grade Students

2004

The People We Love

We would like to dedicate this book to our friends and family who inspire us to read, write, and love words!

MRS. ROBERTSON'S FIRST GRADE CLASS

My parents show they love me by taking me to Carowinds and sometimes Cherry Park. They take me to the Pineville Mall. People love me when they do nice things for me, like on my birthday they took me to a really big mall. They bought me clothes and other stuff. They hug me every night, well almost. Sometimes my sisters and me play games like ball. I throw the ball to her and she throws it to me. That's love.

By Jair Hernandez

***

The People I love are my parents because they take me down to the park where I play football. They kiss me everyday when my mom gets home from work. My mom lays with my brother trying to get him to go to sleep. He's only four. My family helps me find my Scooby Doo when it's time to go to bed. We also help my brother find his orange teddy he got at Wal-Mart. That is love when you help each other. My parents took my brother and me to Disney World. We went in the Haunted Mansion. I was like "Hey you monsters, wanna piece of me". My parents took me on a trip I will never forget, that is love.

By JT Stegall

***

The People I love are my dad's mom. She loves me a lot. I go to her house every time and I get to see her a long time. We like her food. We sleep downstairs and she sleeps upstairs because her bed is up there. We take a bath if she says we have too. We meet her at McDonalds and we go to church. I love my mom, dad, and my sister. I really love my new baby brother. He whines a lot, but I still love him. I get to hold him sometimes. I really love my Maw Maw and Paw Paw too. We go to there house and play. They have a lot of toys. I spend the night with them all the time. We play games with Paw Paw. My Maw Maw likes to watch TV with me. Sometimes the people I love call me Bear because they like to snuggle with me.

By Lauren Wells

***

My Mommy and my Daddy love me so does my Aunt Tang and Grandmaw. My Aunt Pat loves me too. My mom buys me clothes and my dad plays football with me. My Aunt Tang loves me because I clean up her yard. She gives me ice cream and helps me with my homework. My Grandmaw fixes the best food for me. She bought me a truck for Christmas. My Aunt Pat loves me because she hugs me and I help her clean up the house. All these people I love are my family.

By Ebasion Moore

***

The people I love are my Grandma Alma, my Grandma Nody, Grandma Punkin, and Grandma Ann. I love my mom too. Grandma Alma takes me to the park and sometimes she takes me to her church. Grandma Nody picks me up from my mama's house and takes me to the basketball game. Grandma Punkin lets me help her clean up and sometimes she takes me to my Uncle Paul's house to see my cousins. On Friday I went up to my Grandma Ann's house and we had went to the park where she had got married at and went to go get some ice cream. My mom helps me with my homework and she helps me clean my room up when it's a mess. I love these people because they do good things to make me feel good.

By Dienikque Brown

***

I love my mom, my dad, my "Me Me", my Becky, and my grandpa. I know my mom loves me because when I am good at school she lets me have candy. My dad loves me because he doesn't fuss at me. My "Me Me" loves me because she gives me a lot of stuff and she gives me money when I do stuff for her. Becky loves me because she plays with me a lot and she is not rough with me. My grandpa loves me because he takes me to Lake Wylie to ride horses. I know these people love me because they take me somewhere special and give me money and stuff.

By Alex Lewis

***

My Daddy loves me because he lets me sit on his lap and he lets me hug him and he feeds me my favorite food and always takes care of me. My Mom loves me because she don't let us run into the road by ourselves. My sister Deanna loves me because she lets me sleep in her bed sometimes and whenever my mom tells her to watch me she does and takes care of me. And me and her, we wanted to get a suntan, but we were so hot we couldn't take it no more. My brother Austin loves me. He plays house with me and he plays trucks and cars with me.

By Kara Heffner

***

I love my Daddy because he got me a swing and easel. I love my Maw Maw because she bakes cookies for me and in the summer she is going to let me help her in the garden and she's going to help me with the pond and she's even going to buy me more fish. I love my grandpa because he helps me on the computer. I love my grandma Elaine because she helps me with my homework and helps me get on the Internet and buys me a lot of stuff. I love my doggie named Gizmo because he is going to be a good summer dog and I get to play with him a lot. I love my Aunt Jennifer because she takes me to church with her all the time. I love my cousins because they come and see me. My cousins love me because I give them my shoes that I can't fit in anymore. I love my friend Marlene because she gets off the bus with me. I love my teacher because she teaches me how to do math and lots of stuff. I love my friends because they play with me a lot.

By Destiny Hansen

✵✵✵

I love my Aunt Tiffany because on Friday she always comes and gets me from my house. We go get something to eat from Jack N The Box. I liked the burgers and French-fries. We go to the park and play games. My Daddy loves me too. At Christmas time he always buys me clothes. My mom takes me to Myrtle Beach or Carowinds when school gets out. My mom always fixes me peanut butter and jelly sandwich or apples and oranges after school. I love these people because they give me stuff I want and take me places.

By Tyeisha McKnight

✵✵✵

I think my mama loves me because I be good. Also because I listen at school. I almost be good every day. My step-dad Trip loves me too. He loves me because I always be good for him. I do what he says. My grandma Jill love me because I help her clean up her barn and because I help her cook supper and dinner and breakfast. My real dad loves me too. I know he loves me because he be nice to me. My grandma Shari loves me because I bring her treats. I love her because I go see her all the time.

By Kris Mackey

***

Love is something that when people give you stuff. They take you shopping. I love my mom and my dad and my brother. We show each other we love each other by playing games, we go outside and ride our bikes, and we go to a restaurant. We eat and talk a lot. My brother plays with my mama a lot, too. I talk to my dad. Me and my brother play while my mama and daddy go get ice cream. I watch my brother until they come back. That is love in my family.

By Asia Grant

***

Love is when you take care of people. Like if you was their mama you would take care of them. My mom helps my grand-mama clean up her house and gives her money. She does a lot of things for her. My mom loves me because she didn't want to buy me a dog for my birthday, but she did. She paid a lot of money for her. My mom buys toys and stuff for me. My Ma loves me too. She's my mama's mama. She makes cakes for me for my birthday. Her daughter plays with me too. I love my cousin Jasmine because she plays with me a lot. She is three years old.

By Iman Crawford

***

Love is like when you care about people. I know that my daddy loves my mom because he lives with her. He stays home with her and buys her stuff. My mom loves him because she hugs him. My mom takes me places and she lets us go whereever we want to go. Mom buys me clothes. She always makes sure I'm dressed every morning. When I go to bed she hugs me every night.

By Talasia Thompson

***

My mama loves me because she gives me toys and she hugs me. She takes me to stores and she gives me sugar and that's the end. I love Michael because I sit on his lap and play with him.

By Alex Phillips

***

I know my mom loves me because she give me stuff like toys, games, clothes, and shoes. She gives me food like pizza, hamburgers, and French fries. I love my daddy. He plays with me.

By Devante' Thompson

***

I love my grandma because she takes me places and she makes me stuff. I love mom because she makes me my favorite food, macaroni and cheese. We go special places. I love my dad because he lets me sit on his lap and watch TV. I love my little brother because he plays with me. I love my family because they first loved me.

By Mark Conoly

***

I love my mom. She buys me stuff for school. My baby brother cause he swings with me. I love my NiNi cause she bought me a purple bike for my birthday. My sister cause she rides bikes with me. My uncle TJ plays cards with me. My other brother because he plays Playstation II with me.

By Marlene Davis

***

I love my daddy and my mommy because they tuck me in sometimes. I love my Paw Paw too!

By Ray Palmer

***

Roses are red and violets are blue. The flag is the same color too!

By Ali Williams

***

By Denae Lane

MRS. HAMMOND'S FIRST GRADE CLASS

A Loving Family
Someone in my family is sick everyday. But I still love my family everyday and they love me too.
By Ke'Lazia Lytle

✳✳✳

Aunt Teresa
My Aunt Teresa takes me to school. When it's time to go to school we show each other love by hugging.
By Candice Wilkerson

✳✳✳

My Family
I was a maid when my family was sick. I picked up the plates. I picked up tissues and trash. I love my family.
By Shelby Martin

✳✳✳

My Sick Sister
When My sister was sick I helped her by putting her clothes up. When she felt better I helped her with her math. I love my sister.
By Seralysa White

✳✳✳

Helping My Family
I helped my big sister with her math. My sister helped me when I was sick. I helped my mawmaw with the dishes.
By Taylor Porter

***

My Dog
My dog loves me. My dog can give me a high-five. He likes to dance. My dog puts up one paw and then his other paw. I love my dog.
By Andrew Sims

***

My Mommy
When my mommy was sick I felt her head and I took her temperature. I got her a glass of water. She felt much more better.
By Brantley Donahue

***

Birthdays (a poem)
Birthdays are sweet.
Sweet, just like me.
Cake.
I like to eat the cake.
By Lucius Greene

***

Sick
My daddy took care of me when I was sick. I had a 25 hour virus!
By Chasity Lee

***

How I Love My Grandaddy

I help my grandad. I put cover on him. I get him a kleenex. I help him all the time.

By Sa'Daja Sanders

***

Sharing Love

We can share love by hugging each other and making people happy. When people are sad you can make them happy again.

By Sasha McConnell

***

My Stepdad

When my stepdad was sick I did the dishes. I played with him. I brought his books. I love my stepdad.

By Matthew Hayner

***

My Family

My family loves me and I love them. My family feeds me. My family plays games with me. They let me choose what to watch. They let me choose what to listen to. They care for me and I care for them. They love me and I love them.

By Charles Jackson

MS. CAPP'S FIRST GRADE CLASS

"Friendship"
The two animal friends went out to play around a tree until the leopard showed up. Everyone ran inside the tree. The leopard couldn't find them. The leopard looked all around. He still couldn't find them. He goes away and they lived happily ever after.
By Melia Burley and Haley Boheler

***

"Best Friends"
Once upon a time there were two butterflies. One butterfly was crying. The other one said, "What's wrong?" "I am sad because I have no friends," said Rachel. Jimmy said, "I will be your friend." They flew together. They played together. Jimmy said, "I had so much fun." "Me, too," said Rachel. "Do you want do something else?" He said, "Okay." So they played together some more. They had so much fun. They were best friends.
By Harley Russell and Brianna Carter

***

"My Grandparents"
My Grandpa went to work. I said bye. I played with my Grandma. I love my Grandma.
By David Blauvelt

***

"My Mom"

I like playing with my Mom in the snow. We have fun together. She plays with my dog and me. We throw snowballs. My mom is so much fun.

By Austin Hall

***

"Sledding With My Mom"

Once upon a snowy day, I had a snowball fight with my mom. We made a snowman. We bought a sled. My mom and I went sledding in the snow. We went down a hill. It was fast. We had fun in the snow.

By Khaliaha McConnell

***

"The Summer Day"

One day my mom and I were walking down the street. My mom asked, "Do you want to swim?" I said, "Yes!" So I went home and put on my bathing suit. We went in the pool and swam and splashed and made a whirlpool. We got out and ate lunch. I ate a bologna sandwich and chips. Then we ran and jumped in the pool again. It was the best summer day.

By Kinsleigh Pilot

MRS. JETER'S FIRST GRADE CLASS

Love is when somebody cares about you.
When I think of love I think about my family.
By Bailey Falls

***

Love is when you go and get married to another person.
Love is when somebody tells you they love you and they
want to go and play with you.
When I think of love I think of God.
By Nicholas Norman

***

Love is when you like somebody.
Love is when people love each other.
When I think of love I think about girls.
By Nicholas Carter

***

Love is a family.
Love is when you have friends.
When I think of love I think of kisses.
By Lauren Jones

***

Love is when you have a crush on somebody.
Love makes you think you love your parents.

When I think of love I think of my family.
By Kelci Connelly

***

Love is when you love your parents.
Love is when you have a girlfriend.
When I think of love I think about my girlfriend.
By Matthew Ducharme

***

Love is when you have a crush on somebody.
Love is when you love your family.
When I think of love I think of everybody and that everybody loves each other.
By Rebecca Robinson

***

Love is when you want to get married to your girlfriend.
Love is when you want to keep something and you don't want to give it away.
When I think of love I think about getting married.
By Lewantrae Brown

***

Love is when you like somebody a lot and hug them.
Love is when you get married.
When I think of love I think about my mommy.
By Austin Snyder

***

Love is when you don't fight.
Love is when you say good words to people.

Love is when you are not mean.
When I think of love I think about nice people.
By Tyler Stone

***

Love is when your mom says, "I love you."
I feel good when people say, "I love you."
When I think of love I think of my mom and dad.
By Telly Pettus

***

Love is when you like somebody and they like you too.
Love is when somebody takes you out to eat at Outback.
When I think of love I think of my mom and dad.
By Sara Mitchell

***

Love means that you love people in your family and your
friends.
Love makes you feel happy.
When I think of love I think of my mother and my daddy.
By Amber Edwards

***

Love is when you love your pets.
Love makes you feel funny.
When I think of love I think of my grandmom and my
granddad.
By Tybreesha Baxter

***

Love means that you love your family.
You can fall in love with somebody.
Love is in your heart.
When I think of love I think about my family.
By Joel Beasley

***

Love makes me feel happy.
Love is when you hug somebody.
When I think of love I think of my mom and my dad.
By Monica Moore

***

Love is when you love your whole family.
When somebody tells me that they love me then I feel I am loved.
Love makes you feel good.
When I think of love I think about my grandmother.
By Antonia Williams

***

Love is when you get married.
When I think about love I think about girls.
By Brandon Vang

by Torri Valderrama

MRS. TUCKER'S FIRST GRADE CLASS

Love
Love means something you do for your family and friends. I love my family because they care for me. I love my friends because they make me feel happy when I am sad. Love means that you care for one another. Love means being sweet. Love means you care for people that take care of you. They take care of you because they want you to have a great life when you grow up. They care for you because they love you a lot. They make you happy because they take care of you. When I am loved I feel happy.
By Sarah Moss

✳✳✳

Love
I love my mom because she takes care of us. I love my dad because he loves me. Love is caring. Love makes me happy.
By Russell Blauvelt

✳✳✳

What is Love?
Love is when you hug each other. I love my dog. I love my mom and dad. I love my brother and sister. I love my friends and my pets. I love my teacher. And I love pizza, too. But I don't hug pizza.
By Patrick Marhan

✳✳✳

What is Love?

Love is when people love each other. Love is when people buy ice cream for each other. My dad loves us and he buys us ice cream everyday.

By Lizzie Passmore

***

What is Love?

Love is when you get married. Love is when you kiss and take care of each other. My parents love each other. They take care of us because they got married. My parents are happy and they make me happy. They cook food for us, and they are nice to me and my brother. I help mom set the table and I help my dad with his wheelchair. This is how we take care of each other. Love is when your pets are nice. I feed my cats so they won't die. My brother and I like to play with our dog. Our pets love us because we take care of them. Live is really good. I makes us take care of each other and it makes us feel good.

By Kirsta Needham

***

What is Love?

Love is when your parents love you and give you stuff. They always help you do your homework. They keep you healthy and clean. Your pets also take care fo you and make you feel happy when you're afraid. Your teacher takes care of you a lot and makes you smart and brave. Your friends take care of you and they make you happy. Your friends like to have fun with you. I love my parents very much because they give me food every day and night. Parents hug you every time you get on the bus. They kiss you good night and hug you in the morning. You have to love your parents because they love you a lot. Your aunts and uncles love you. Your cousins do, too. Everybody in your family loves you.

By Katherine Wilkins

✳✳✳

What is Love?

Love is when you fall in love. You might get married. Sometimes you might get a baby. You might have two kids. You love each other forever.

By Evan Danenhower

✳✳✳

What is Love?

Love is all about loving your mom. And you can love your dad. And I wish my granddad didn't die. I wish one day my grandma wouldn't die. I love God and Jesus. I love my whole family. Love is all about loving everybody.

By Diamond Sanders

✳✳✳

What is Love?

Love is when you care about people. I care about my mom and my dad and my brother. I care about my whole family, and they care about me. Love is when you play with your friends and your family. Whe have a good time together. We play games and watch T.V. together. We play ball, too. Love is when you love someone and you are happy.

By Deshaw Andrews

✳✳✳

What is Love?

Love is when you care about someone. You make them

happy and they make you happy, too. Love is when somebody is hurt, and you can show love with cards and flowers or any other thing, too. My aunts and uncles love me just like they love their little boys and girls. And our moms and dads love us, too. You love your sisters and brothers. You love your dogs and cats, too. I love God and Jesus, too. Love can be fun.

By Denae Lane

***

What is Love?

Love is when you have love in your heart. And you are caring. Mom and Dad love me and they respect me. And my brother. We love each other and we play together. I have love in my family. I care for my mom, my dad, and my little brother.

By Chelsey Herring

***

What is Love?

Love is when you love your mommies and daddies. Love makes new friends. That makes me giggle. I love my mommy and daddy. Love is caring about somebody else.

By Cameron Garner

***

What is Love?

Love is when you love somebody. You do good things for them and they do good things for you. I hope my mom wash the dishes and she helps me take care of myself. Love makes me feel good. I feel safe when I am loved. I feel glad that my mom feeds me and takes care of me. So love is what protects me.

By Brandon Lockridge

***

What is Love?

Love is when people love you. Love is when you love somebody. You will get married. And you will kiss the bride. I love you and you love me, too.

By Autumn Bailey

***

Love

Love is very special to my family. Love is when you're in love with somebody. Everyone has a person to love. I love my mom. I love me, too.

By Adam Mills

***

Love

Love is about your family. I love my family and my dogs. I love my brother. Me and my family go camping. You can show love when you get someone hearts, chocolates, and presents. You can fall in love. When I get older, I will have a girlfriend. And you have to date. Then you get married, and you have a family of your own. That is love.

By Wesley Mitchell

***

What is Love?

Love is good and nice. Love is when your mom and dad love you, and you love them, too. I love my teacher and she loves me. Your mom and dad care about you, and they want you to be healthy. Your pets love you and you love them. You love your family and they love you. Your brothers make you happy a lot. Love is pretty and good and nice. Love makes us happy.

By Torri Valderrama

***

What is Love?

Love is caring for people and bringing money to the children that have cancer and leukemia. Parents can love you, and other people can love you too. They always help you do your homework. They keep you healthy and clean. Your pets also love you and can play with you.

By Tony Turner

***

What is Love?

Love is everybody! Love people that are sick and have leukemia. Pray for them is they don't have love. What is love? Love is important. That's why God gave us love. Everybody loves you. Angels love you, God loves you. Your mom, dad, sister, and brother love you. I love my pet and my uncle and aunt. XXOO. If you be nice and kind, you might get love. When you love, it might make you happy. I always makes me happy. Love is when your mom and dad kiss you good night. Love is caring about somebody that has a broke bone or that is sick. How does love make you feel?

By Taylr Sharp

MS. KOTULA'S FIRST GRADE CLASS

What is Love?
by Zachary Thrift
Love is driving me to school and love is playing board games with me.
Love is teaching me to walk and teaching me to read.
I show my mom I love her by being good.
My mom shows me she loves me by taking me to the beach.
Love is when my cat licks me.

***

What is Love?
by Mary Lyn Mitchell
Love is when my family cooks dinner together.
Love is when my Grandma and Paw-Paw take me to Missouri and to Florida.
Love is when my mom and dad tuck me in at night.
Love is when my mom and I take turns reading at night.
Love is when my brother, my mom, and my dad play with me.
Love is when my mom and dad help me with my homework.
Love is when my mom and dad kiss and hug me.
Love is when I sleep with my daddy.
I show my mom I love her by helping her clean up the kitchen after dinner.

I show my dad I love him by holding the door when he is unlocking the door.
I show my brother I love him by not fighting with him.
I show my teacher love by working hard.
I show my soccer coach love by hustling.
I show my Grandma and Paw-Paw love by helping in the garden.

**

What is Love?
by Hylah Miller
Love is when my mama kisses me and hugs me morning and night.
Love is when my friends play with me at recess.
Love is when my friend plays with me in the pool.
Love is when my grandma and pa-pa take me to Disney.
Love is when my friend plays with me at my mom's work.
Love is when I hold my baby brother.
Love is when my mama gets me toys.
Love is when my mama takes me to ride in the red car.
Love is when my friend Jhona plays board games with me like Scooby Doo, matching game, and the Wizard of Oz.
Love is when my mama tucks me in the bed.
Love is when my mama helps me with my homework.
Love is when my mama buys me clothes.

**

What is Love?
by Thomas Shirley
Love is driving me to the store and lots of other places.
Love is helping me do my homework.
Love is telling me how to spell words.

Love is giving me a lot of money.
Love is teaching me the letters.
Love is buying houses for me.
Love is cooking food for me.
Love is drawing pictures for me.
I show my mom and dad that I love them by giving them hugs and kisses.
I love my mom and dad by helping with dinner.
I love my mom and dad by setting the table.
Love is when my mom and dad wash my clothes.
Love is when my mom and dad buy food for me.

***

What is Love?
by Amber Hoyt
My sister loves me because she lets me play with her toys.
My family loves me because they bought me a dog.
My dog loves me because she licks me.
My mommy loves me because she is nice to me.
My dad loves me because he hugs me.

***

What is Love?
by Taylor Clabough
Love is when you love other people and love your family. Love your family every day. People love you every time you are good and love is when other people love you too. Love is when your family loves you. My dad shows me that he loves me by playing with me. My mommy shows me that she loves me by cooking supper. My mommy shows me by taking me to school.

***

What is Love?

by Robert Marhan

Love is when you get gifts and my mom and dad buy me gum. My mom cooks me dinner. They get me a dog and a bed. My mom lets me get ice cream and a bike. I give my mom and dad hugs and kisses. My dad's friend built me a picnic table. I tell my mom and dad I love them when they are sleeping. My mom buys me school stuff so I can learn. My mom and dad buy me books. My sister lets me borrow her stuff. My teacher lets me do fun stuff to learn. My mom and dad buy me hats and cake. My brother plays tag with me. This is what love is.

***

What is Love?

by Jake Boone

Love is when your family is having fun together.

Love is when you are hugging.

Love is when your little brother is having fun playing with you.

Love is when your mom makes you cookies.

Love is when your cousin and you watch TV together.

***

What is Love?

by Andruw Means

Love is when my mom and maw-maw drive me to school every day.

Love is when my mom gives me hugs and kisses every morning and night.

Love is when I help my mom and when I take care of her.

Love is when my mom teaches me new stuff.

Love is when my baby sister hugs me a lot.

Love is when my mom tucks me in bed.

Love is when my mom and maw maw hugs and kisses me a lot of times.

Love is when I kiss my mom a lot of times.

Love is when my mom taught me how to walk when I would fall down.

***

What is Love?

by Kiyanna Robinson

I love my mom for getting me gifts. I love my dad because he loves me. Love is having friends. Love is my baby brother. My teacher loves me because she tells me and I love her. I love Megan and Mary Lyn because they are my friends.

***

What is Love?

by Megan Burley

Love to me is my mom and daddy.

Love to me is my family and friends.

Love to me is when my sister plays with me.

Love to me is helping my mom.

Love to me is taking me to the store.

Love to me is showing my mom my clean room.

Love to me is my teacher.

Love to me is my dog and cat.

***

What is Love?

by Antonio Bantum

Love is when my mom plays with me.

Love is when my dad helps me.

I show my mom I love her by saying "I love you."
Love is when my dog licks me.
Love is when my aunt picks me up and puts me in the air.

***

What is Love?
by Anthony Allen
Love is when my mom hugs me.
Love is when people give me Valentines.
I love my family and my family loves me.
Love is celebrating Valentine's Day.
Love is when my mom helps me with my work.
I love my teacher Ms. Kotula.
I love me too.
I love my dog and her name is Sandy,
My family is nice to me like Ms. Kotula.

***

What is Love?
by Brianna Clabaugh
Love is when my mom turns my TV on and it is high.
Love is when she pushes me on the swings.
Love is when Ms. Kotula teaches me how to learn.
Love is when I give my mom and dad a card.
Love is when I give my mom and dad kisses.
Love is when my mom and dad take me to Kansas.
Love is when my family takes me to Carowinds.
Love is when I hug my mom and dad.

***

What is Love?
by Taylor Ramsey

Love is when my mommy and daddy take me to the store and to the beach and almost everywhere.

Love is when my friend Haley and I play together.

Love is when I get to see my baby sister at daycare when we leave school.

Love is when I get to help my mommy in the kitchen.

Love is when I get to help my mommy with my baby sister at home.

Love is when I get to help my mommy remember things when we go out somewhere.

Love is when I do not bother my baby sister at home.

Love is when I clean my room at home.

Love is when my mommy and daddy give me gifts.

Love is when my mommy and daddy got married.

***

What is Love?

by Logan Carter

Love is when my mom and dad take me on vacations.

Love is when my mom and dad taught me how to ride a bike. When I fell down, she helped me up.

I think my mom and dad love me in a special way.

Love is when somebody teaches you something like Ms. Kotula teaches us lots of stuff.

Love is when my mom and dad help me on my homework.

Love is when my mom and dad take me to Virginia to see my cousins.

Love is when my mom makes dinner for me.

Love is when my mom takes me to school.

Love is when my mom tucks me in at night.

Love is when my mom and dad give me gifts.

Love is when my mom gives me kisses.

***

What is Love?

by Malachi Brown

Love is when my mom would teach me how to walk every time I would fall down and my mom would help me up. My mom takes me around the park. My mom gives me hugs and kisses. Love makes people happy. My mom cooks me great food like vegetables and fruits. Love is when my mom helps me make up my bed and I help her make up her bed. I help my mom cook eggs. She helps me read stories. She is nice to me. She makes me happy by playing games with me. She takes me for walks. Love is when my sisters help me do my homework. Love is when I teach my baby brother how to talk real nice.

***

What is Love?

by Rachel Petty

Love is family love.

Love is hugs and kisses.

Love is a silent swan.

Love is your mommy and daddy playing the basketball game horse with you.

Love is a special gift.

Love is holding your baby brother.

Love is buying me toys.

Love is when I bought a toy fire truck that costs two dollars.

Love is hugging your grandmama.

Love is kissing your granddaddy.

Love is playing with me.

Love is cooking for me.

Love is playing.

Love is sending a love letter.
Love is loving other people.

***

What is Love?
by Quazenia Weaver
Love is your mom.
Love is your family.
Love is your daddy and your sisters.
Love is getting me something for Christmas.
Love is playing games with me.
Love is reading bed stories to me.
Mrs. Sims' First Grade Class

Love is about...
Love is about who you love. I love my Mom and Dad because they are nice. Love to me is hugging and kissing.
By Jevante Floyd

***

People I Love
We love our families. I love my Dad and my Mom and my sister. I love my cats. My family loves me too. To show love, I help my sister and do something with her like play a game.
By Daniel Bradley

***

What is Love?
Love is when you kiss and hug someone. I love my Maw Maw and I love my Mom. I love my brothers. I play with them. Love is hugging or giving presents.
By Sydney Burton

***

Love

I love my Mom and she loves me back. She loves me by giving me food and love.

By Tykevious brown

***

What is Love?

Love is something you take care of. Love is kissing someone and giving them presents. Love is also when show someone respect. Love is being nice.

Lyric Gwinn

***

Love

Love is caring. Love is helping. Love is kissing. Love is hugging. I love my mom, my dad, and my brother.

Princess Murchison

***

Love Is

Love is caring for each other. Love is when you marry and spend time together with someone. That is what I think love is.

Brittany Lawrence

***

Love

Love is when you have a crush on someone. You can also show them manners. And you can be kind. Love is when you respect a person. Love is when you help him or her.

By Tyler McCabe

✲✲✲

Love

Love means you love someone in your life. Love means you like them. Love is respectful. Love is caring and helping. I love my Mom.

By Lydia Gabbard

✲✲✲

What I love

I love my dog. He is a black lab, and his name is Sparky. He likes me. I show him I love him by petting him and playing with him. I love my dog.

By Brandon Carden

✲✲✲

People I Love

I love my Mommy because she is nice to me. And she is a good person to me. She loves me and that is why I love her. I really, really love her too. Just like she really loves me. And just like she really loves her family too.

By Heather Via

✲✲✲

Love

I love my Mommy. I love my sister. Love is hugging and kissing and being nice. I love my family.

By Brittany Sizemore

✲✲✲

What is Love

What is love? Love is something that is special. And it makes you feel special. It makes you feel like hugging and kissing. That is love.

By Kaitlyn Bell

***

Love

Love is when we love our family. I can show my family that I love them by kissing and hugging them. I can show Snoopy love by playing with him. I can show my Aunt I love her by helping to wash clothes and being nice. I can show the baby love by feeding him. I love my whole family.

By Megan Sutphin

***

Love
Love is sweet.
Love is nice.
Love is cute.
Love is butterflies.
Love is very kind.
Love is loving my best friend, Megan.
Love.
By BreAnna Swick

***

MS. JOHNSON'S SECOND GRADE CLASS

Seth and Me

He is helpful to me,
He is there when I am not free,

He plays my game,
When I am lame,

We make a run at the sun,
Just for fun,

He knows what I say,
And we play and play,

Together we will always stand,
As long as he is my man.

By Shuler Littleton

***

My Mom is Helpful

She takes me for my allergy shot,
Which I have to take a lot,

She sometimes fixes supper,
And my Dad sometimes calls it rubber.

My Mom is always helping,
Even when I'm yelping.

By Nora Childers

***

My mom is Helpful

My mom is helpful you will see,
She spends a lot of time with me.

She cooks for us,
She won't let us fuss,

She washes my clothes,
And cleans my nose,

My mom is helpful to me.

Octravion Mandrek

***

My Brother is Fun

My brother likes the Fall,
Because he plays a lot of basketball,

My brother likes to ride his bike,
He takes me on his hikes,

My brother likes to fly a kite,
When we play we leaf fight
By Laura Saboley

***

My Grandma's the Best

My Grandma was a fantastic and special person to my dad, and me.
She said I was the best grandson she ever had,
She's in a better place now.

By Cas Johnson

***

Cas Johnson

My Mom

She helps me do my homework when I get stuck,
She taught me to drink out of a cup,

She always cook,
And she helps me read books.
By Lane Smith

***

My Dad

My daddy is fun because he shows me how to play base-
ball,
And the fun sports like basketball and football,

My Dad shows me things at the zoo,
And takes care of me when I get a terrible flu.

By Hamilton McGarity

***

My Brother is Funny

My brother likes me as a sister,
So he tries to make me laugh by saying, "Good-day Mis-
ter."

Autumn Gorham

***

Love bug

My grandma is so sweet,
She always has a treat,

For me and her to share,
I really can not bear.

We both have a bird,
It really is a nerd,

We both like to miss,
And give a little kiss.

By Annah Whitehead

***

My Nana

My nana lets me play,
Almost everyday,

My nana shares with me,
Almost everything she sees,

She buys me everything,
And she loves to hear me sing.
By Kat Logue

***

My Grandma's Nice

My grandma's nice because she gives us stuff,
But sometimes she looks rough,

My grandma's nice because she tells us what she did,
Even when she was a kid,

Then we ask her what she saw,
She said, "A lady wearing a shawl".
By Payton Hollis

***

My Sister

My sister gives my dog his feed,
And helps me to read,

She plays with him so I can go free,
And helps me find my key,

She helps me with my hair,
And has a favorite bear,

She also helps me pick out my clothes,
And she doesn't pick her nose.
By Katie Lackey

***

My Dad

When I cry my dad cheers me up,
He makes my brother feed the pup,

He is fun when he picks me up from school,
He might even buy me a big fat pool.

By Grace Whitson

***

My Dad

My dad is always sweet,
When he leaves he gives me a treat,

He's so sweet you see,
That's why he loves me.

By Sammie McClurkin

***

My Dad

My dad is the coolest Dad,
He makes me laugh when I am sad,

He helps me with my homework,
And helps me with my football work.
By Josh Rolan

***

My Mom

My mom has a hat,
That she puts on the cat,

It looks very funny,
She likes it when it's sunny,

When I am sick she takes care of me,
And when I need help with homework
she is there for me.

By Tyler Reinhart

*** *

My Dad

I care about my dad,
When he is sad,

He cares about me when I am sad,
And when I am mad.

By JoJo Strikey

*** *

My Mom

I have diabetes and my mom helps me,
She brings me to school everyday you will see,

She helps my sister and brother too,
Who never complains? My mom, that's who?

By Alicia Eyler

www.ingramcontent.com/pod-product-compliance
Lightning Source LLC
Chambersburg PA
CBHW071124280526
45787CB00003B/1154